What If?

By Pauline Cartwright
Illustrated by Colby Heppell

Pearson Australia
(a division of Pearson Australia Group Pty Ltd)
707 Collins Street, Melbourne, Victoria 3008
PO Box 23360, Melbourne, Victoria 8012
www.pearson.com.au

First published 2012 by Pearson Australia
2017 2016 2015 2014
10 9 8 7 6 5 4 3 2

Publisher: Sabine Bolick
Project Editor: Suzy Freeman
Editor: Kerry Nagle
Designer: Jennifer Johnston
Copyright & Pictures Editor: Marg Barber
Illustrator: Colby Heppell
Printed and bound in Australia by Pegasus Media & Logistics

ISBN 978 1 4425 3771 2

Pearson Australia Group Pty Ltd ABN 40 004 245 943

Contents

Chapter 1

Something Bad

COOPER WAS SHY. It took a long time for him to feel comfortable with new people and places. He didn't like speaking in front of the class. He didn't like sudden surprises, either. They made him feel worried.

Today at school, he'd had a sudden surprise. After school, he ran down the footpath towards home. His stomach churned in a very uncomfortable way. He burst through the door of his house.

"Mum! Mum!"

His mother looked up. She was helping his little sister, Angie, change her clothes for dance class.

"Cooper!" she said. "You gave me a fright!" Then she smiled. "Did something exciting happen at school?"

"No!" panted Cooper. "No! Something really bad happened!"

His mother gave a small frown. "You're not just getting upset about something that's not worth it, are you, Cooper?"

"No!" Cooper protested. "Something bad did happen. Our class is going to camp! I can't go!"

"Why not?" asked Angie.

Cooper started to answer but his mother put her hand up, like a traffic officer.

"No, we'll talk about it later. We have to get Angie to dancing."

In the car, while Mum and Angie chatted about dancing, thoughts flew around Cooper's mind.

"**What if** I get sick on the bus going to camp?" he thought. "**What if** I get sick at camp? **What if** I have to share a room with Johnno Rush?" Johnno was the loudest boy in their class and he sometimes teased Cooper and laughed at him. "**What if** I can't sleep at night? **What if** I get bitten by a snake? **What if** ... **What if** ... **What if** ...?"

His mother's voice cut into his thoughts.

"Cooper, let's have a milkshake after we've dropped off Angie. You can tell me all about the camp then."

At the café, Mum bought a cappuccino and a raspberry milkshake.

"Now," she said, "tell me why you can't go to camp."

All the **what-ifs** in Cooper's head began tumbling out.

"What if I don't like what's for dinner and I get hungry? What if we have to play soccer? I'm no good at soccer. What if everyone laughs at me?"

"Cooper," began Mum, but Cooper wasn't listening.

"And Ms Rivani said we'll all help out in the kitchen. What if I can't peel potatoes? What if it's pitch black at night and there are no lights on and I can't find the toilets? What if—"

"Stop right there, Cooper," said Mum in a very firm voice. "Drink your milkshake."

Cooper stared at her for a moment. Then he began to drink.

"Cooper," Mum's voice was still very firm, so Cooper didn't dare to interrupt, "I have often told you that your what-if questions aren't helpful. You will love camp if you stop worrying about things that will probably never happen."

"They *might* happen," muttered Cooper. He was frowning. "I just don't want to go."

"Liam will be going," his mother reminded him.

Cooper nodded. Liam was his best friend.

"And Alice from next door, and Grant, Nasib and Mika," his mother went on.

They were all classmates that Cooper played with.

Cooper frowned some more. "What if my friends don't—"

"Cooper!" His mother spoke sharply. "No **what-ifs**! Not one more!" She put an arm around Cooper's shoulders. "Cooper, camp will be really fun. I'm sure about that, so stop worrying."

Chapter 2

Grandad's Trick

OVER THE NEXT FEW WEEKS, Cooper's teacher, Ms Rivani, told the class about the camp, which was near an old gold-mining town. They would be away for three nights and four days. She wrote a list of the activities on the board.

- panning for gold
- visiting an old mine
- lessons in an "olden-days" school
- museum visit
- nature hike

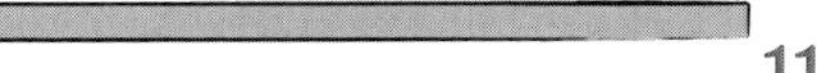

"There will also be time to relax and play games," she said. "And you will all write about your experiences in a journal."

The planned activities made more **what-ifs** swirl in Cooper's head until he felt dizzy. But he kept them to himself.

At home, his mum chatted cheerfully to him about camp. Cooper grizzled to Angie, "Mum should go on camp herself. I don't want to go."

Angie frowned. "If kinder has a camp, I won't go either."

Cooper was glad when Grandad rang on Saturday and asked him to mow his lawn. Grandad had a push mower with blades that whirred like an egg-beater when Cooper pushed it around Grandad's tiny lawn. Cooper loved chatting and eating chocolate cake with Grandad afterwards.

Grandad said that he had heard about Cooper's school camp. A whole string of what-if questions tumbled out of Cooper.

Then he stopped.

"Sorry! Mum said I wasn't to think about the what-ifs."

Grandad pushed another piece of chocolate cake towards him. "I felt like that the first time I had to go to camp."

"You did?"

"I did," nodded Grandad. "I asked what-if questions for days."

"Really? Like what?"

"What if I don't like the other guys? What if they don't like me? What if I can't keep up when we go hiking? Things like that."

Cooper felt better that Grandad knew how he was feeling.

"Was the camp really bad?" he asked.

"No," said Grandad. "I really liked it. But I found out a good trick before I went."

"What trick?"

"Well, I was a fairly brainy person, like you. I worked out there were two kinds of **what-ifs**, the gloomy sort and the happy sort. 'What if I can't keep up when we're hiking?' was gloomy. But 'What if I'm the best hiker of the bunch?' was happy. The trick was to turn a gloomy what-if into a happy one. I guess you've worked out that trick already."

Cooper nodded slowly. Maybe it wasn't lying if he didn't say anything.

That night, Cooper tried out happy what-if thoughts in bed.

"What if I love the meals because we get dessert every night?" His mouth watered, imagining apple crumble.

"What if we get to swim instead of playing soccer?" Swimming was his favourite sport.

"What if I get to sleep in a cabin with all my best mates?" They could talk for hours in bed after lights-out.

Then Cooper thought of something really exciting.

What if he found some gold?

The next morning, Cooper couldn't wait to share this **what-if** with his mum.

"Mum, what if I—"

"Cooper!"

"Mum, this is a happy what-if! Grandad taught me about them. What if I find some gold? Wouldn't that be awesome?"

"Awesome!" smiled Mum.

There was a lot of planning to do at school before the camp. Cooper tried to keep positive, but gloomy what-ifs still floated into his head. He looked at the photos of the camp on its website.

"What if I have to sleep in that building right next to the bush?" he thought. "A wild animal might get in."

Then he remembered to try a cheerful what-if. "What if I see some wildlife? That would be cool."

Then, the week before they were going to camp, Cooper got a cold. His nose ran, his cheeks were hot and his head was sore.

"No school today! Back to bed," said Mum firmly.

"What if I miss something really important about camp?" sniffed Cooper.

"Was that a happy what-if?" Mum asked. "You need to get rid of that cold or you won't be able to go to camp." She left the room and Cooper snuggled down and shut his eyes.

"Maybe it wouldn't be too bad if my cold does last a long time!" he thought. "Then I won't have to go to camp."

But then he stopped and really thought about it. After all the planning, part of him really wanted to go to camp and do some of the exciting things they had talked about.

Cooper was torn. He didn't know what he wanted to do now.

Chapter 3

Off to Camp

COOPER'S STOMACH was doing flips. It always did when he was nervous. His cold had gone and now he was on the bus driving away from the school gates. All the class, some parent-helpers and Ms Rivani, plus all their bags, were on board. They were on their way to camp!

Cooper sat beside his friend Liam. He looked out the bus window at his mum and Angie getting smaller and smaller as the bus drove away. He wished they had been able to come to camp with him.

It was noisy in the bus. Then the driver put on the radio and they all started singing.

One of Cooper's favourite songs was playing. He joined in and his stomach settled down.

At lunchtime, the bus stopped at a park. Everyone ran in and out of the trees and across the grass, and laughed and yelled a lot before they all sat down together to eat lunch. It was fun.

Then they were back on the bus again. In one more hour they would be at the camp. "**What if** I don't like it?" wondered Cooper. His stomach started to flip again.

Cooper stopped himself from thinking this way. Instead he thought, "**What if** camp is so good, I don't want to go home?"

"We're nearly there," Ms Rivani announced as they drove through a small town. "This is the old gold-mining town."

There was a loud buzz of excitement. Then the bus stopped at an old building and everyone tumbled out.

"Hey," said Cooper, "it looks just like the photos on the website!"

"But bigger and cooler," said Liam.

Everyone followed Ms Rivani across the grass and through a red door into a big hall.

"This is where we'll do a lot of our activities," she told them.

Next, she called out the rooms they were in. Cooper worried that he would miss his name. Then suddenly he heard, "Liam, Mika, Cooper and Grant are in Room 6."

"Phew," he murmured, remembering the room lists they had made at school.

The boys picked up their bags and followed Ms Rivani to Room 6. She told them there would be a night-light on in the hall and in the toilets at the end, if they needed to go at night.

"Can I go now?" asked Cooper.

"Of course," smiled Ms Rivani. "I'll leave you all to settle in. Everyone is to meet up in the hall in half an hour."

By the time he got back to the bedroom, the top bunks had been taken. Cooper didn't mind, especially when Liam leaned down and pointed to the bed underneath his bunk.

The rest of the day flew by in a flash. They were all shown the kitchen and meals area and had afternoon tea. They looked around the camp grounds and were given a list of their chores.

"Oh no," said Liam. "We're doing dishes tonight!"

Cooper groaned. He hated doing dishes.

They were given their journals. There were gaps underneath each activity so they could write about it.

Before dinner, they could play cricket or go swimming in the pool. Cooper chose swimming and stayed in for ages. He floated on his back, looking up at the blue sky and thought, "**What if** I can swim like this every day?"

That night, dinner was Cooper's favourite meal, lasagna. And there was apple crumble for dessert!

"Hey, Liam," said Cooper, remembering Grandad's trick, "**what if** the meals are this good every night?"

After Cooper's group had done the dishes, Ms Rivani sent them all to their rooms to get warm jackets.

"What's happening now? It's supposed to be bedtime," said Cooper, alarmed. He didn't like surprises.

They went outside, crossed the grass and all sat down together away from the buildings.

"Now," said Ms Rivani, "stay silent and look up."

Above them were a million stars, shining and twinkling. Everyone stared and stared. The stars seemed so much brighter than in the city.

Ms Rivani showed them the patterns in the stars that were called constellations. It was awesome.

Later, when they were all in bed and everyone had stopped talking, Cooper shut his eyes. He didn't worry about sleeping away from home. He lay there remembering the millions of stars.

In no time at all he was asleep.

Chapter 4

So Fast

IT WAS FUN waking up in the morning with a roomful of friends to talk to. It was great having a choice of toast, cereal or scrambled eggs for breakfast. Even filling in the journal sheets and doing the group chores wasn't too bad.

Most fun of all, though, was going to the "olden-days" school. Everyone sat at wooden desks in rows and no-one was allowed to talk. The teacher was dressed in clothes from the 1800s. He looked very formal and carried a stick that was called a cane.

First, they had a writing lesson. The teacher wrote on a blackboard with chalk.

They dipped pens into ink and tried to copy the curly letters the teacher had written. It was hard. Sometimes the ink made puddles on the paper.

"**What if** we had to do this every day?" Cooper whispered to Liam.

"Yeah, I'm glad this is only pretend," Liam whispered back.

"No talking!" The teacher banged his cane on the table, pretending to be cross. Everyone jumped and laughed. Cooper and Liam were embarrassed but they laughed along with everyone else.

After lunch in the park, the class went to the gold-mining museum. They watched a film about how men had once mined for gold. They saw real gold—small flakes and gleaming nuggets in cases. Cooper had a turn at holding a heavy, shining nugget.

Then they panned for gold in troughs of water with gravel in the bottom, like a pretend river. Cooper's heart beat faster as he swished the pan around, washing out the gravel, as they had been shown.

That evening, Cooper wrote in his journal.

Day 2

Today I found some tiny specks of gold. Everyone did! We took them back to camp in tiny bottles. Then, a goldminer called Mr Chen came and spoke to us after dinner. He talked about how gold was now found using big machines. I think I might be a goldminer one day.

Cooper thought about his grandad. He couldn't wait to tell him about all the cool things he was doing at camp.

????

The next day, everyone went on a long walk. They carried picture cards of plants, birds and insects. Ms Rivani and a parent helped them match their cards to the real things.

Cooper and his friends were lucky enough to see an echidna ambling through the bushes. They named him Spike.

That evening, they all got to choose one of six different activities for their last day. Cooper chose an activity straight away. He couldn't wait for the morning to come. But he was sad as well. He had been so worried about coming to camp and now he wished that camp wasn't ending. The time had gone by so fast.

Chapter 5

A Small Clink

COOPER WAS IN the gold-panning group with five other students. One of them was Johnno Rush. Cooper decided to keep away from him. Mr Chen, the goldminer, was in charge. They followed him along a river bank, each carrying a pan and a small, folding shovel. They had to choose a place where they thought they might find gold.

After a while, Cooper asked, "Is this a good place, Mr Chen?"

Mr Chen smiled. "Very good!" he said. "See that bend in the river? That will trap any gold washing downstream."

Each student chose a safe place to work beside the river, unfolded their shovels and filled their pans with gravel. Cooper had learned that gold sank to the very bottom of the river. So he dug down deep where gravel met rock. He shovelled it into his pan. Then he swirled it about, letting the gravel wash out.

"You're good at that," said Mr Chen, who was walking up and down watching everyone. Cooper smiled.

There wasn't even a speck of gold in the first three pans Cooper washed. He moved a little upstream and found a rock in the river with a crack in it. He shovelled the gravel out of the crack and scraped out the mud and sand at the bottom with his fingers. He swirled his pan again. His back and arms were getting a bit sore now.

Then he forgot about being tired. Something **gleamed** in the sand left at the bottom of his pan. Cooper swirled his pan again and stared. There was a little trail of tiny specks, like the tail of a comet. And at the end of the trail was . . . a tiny, yellow-brown nugget.

"Mr Chen!" called Cooper. "Mr Chen!"

"Well, well," said the goldminer when he peered into Cooper's pan. "It's big enough to make a noise when you drop it in your bottle. Well done!"

It wasn't anything like the nugget Cooper had held at the museum, but it did make a small **clink** when he carefully put it in his bottle.

"Wow, man!" said Johnno Rush, grinning beside Cooper. "You're rich!"

Cooper grinned back.

Cooper could have stayed all day at the river. But they were leaving for home straight after lunch.

When they were on the bus and on their way home, Cooper said to Liam, "Camp's gone so fast. I can't believe it's over already."

"You didn't really want to go, did you?" Liam asked.

Cooper went red. "Not at first."

"But I bet you're glad you did!" said Liam.

"Definitely!" smiled Cooper.

Chapter 6

A Trick for Angie

WHEN COOPER GOT HOME, he told Mum and Angie how great camp had been.

"I knew you'd enjoy it," said Mum.

Angie frowned. "I thought you didn't want to go," she said.

"But I did go," said Cooper, "and it was cool. Look what I found."

"Is that real gold in there?" asked Angie, staring at the bottle Cooper showed her.

"It's real," said Cooper.

Mum took the little bottle and tipped it sideways, looking at the tiny nugget lying in the cluster of gold specks.

"I never thought you'd be lucky enough to find a nugget," she said.

"Next week, we're doing talks about camp and parents can come to listen," said Cooper. "We're going to speak about the best things that happened at camp."

"Are you speaking?" Mum asked, surprised.

"Yes," answered Cooper. "I'm talking about finding this **awesome** nugget."

"But you don't like talking in front of people," said Angie.

"Well, I've decided that if you really want to share something, it's easy. I'm going to tell Grandad that, just in case he doesn't know that trick."

????

A week later, Cooper heard Angie in the kitchen, talking to their mother.

"I don't want to be in the kinder concert. What if I forget what to do?" she moaned.

Cooper went into the kitchen. "What concert?" he asked.

"We're having a dance concert and I don't want to be in it. What if I forget the steps? What if I fall over and everyone laughs at me?"

Cooper looked at his mother and then back at Angie.

"Do you know there are happy **what-ifs** and gloomy what-ifs?" he asked.

"I don't know what you mean," frowned Angie.

"Well, 'What if I forget the steps' is a gloomy what-if," said Cooper. "But 'What if I *don't* forget a single step' is a happy what-if."

Angie stared at him. "How does that make me feel better?"

"Thinking happy thoughts makes you feel better," Cooper told her. "If you say 'What if I dance really well and everyone claps', doesn't that make you feel good?"

"I guess so," agreed Angie.

"You'll love being in the concert," said Cooper. "I might even come to watch you."

Angie smiled. "Will you?" she asked and she looked at her mother. "Will you come too, Mum?"

"I'd love to come," said Mum.

"What if Grandad comes too!" said Angie, looking excited.

"Great," said Cooper. "That was a happy **what-if**." He looked at Mum. "She learns even faster than me."

"I've got two brainy kids," smiled Mum.